112 Ways to Use
1 lb. of Ground Beef

Printed in the United States of America
by G&R Publishing Co.

Published By:

507 Industrial Street
Waverly, IA 50677

ISBN-13: 978-1-56383-282-6
ISBN-10: 1-56383-282-8
Item #7027

Table of Contents

With the help of this cookbook, you can whip up 112 delicious family meals. All you'll need is your always-on-hand ingredient: One pound of ground beef.

Beefing Up Your Knowledge:

The Basics of Ground Beef

One pound of ground beef is a great staple for any meal. It's quick, easy, economical and, most of all, tasty! Before you begin preparing your beefy dish, read through these basics about ground beef and discover how to get the most out of your meat.

Types of Ground Beef:

A package of ground beef is generally labeled with its percentage of lean meat. You will notice numbers such as 90/10, 85/15, 80/20 and 75/25. The higher number is the percentage of lean meat, the lower number is the percentage of fat. Leaner meat tends to be drier when cooked, but is lower in fat and calories.

Purchasing Ground Beef:

- Ground beef should be purchased on or before the listed "sell by" date. It should be used or frozen within two days of being purchased.
- When shopping for ground beef, to avoid cross contamination*, choose packages that are sealed tightly and feel cold. Make ground beef one of the last items

you pick up and try to separate it from other items in your cart or bag so juices from the meat do not drip on other foods.

- According to the National Cattlemen's Beef Association, ground beef goes through a number of color changes during its shelf-life. A bright cherry-red color indicates fresh ground beef. A darker purple-red is common in vacuum-packaged ground beef and when the interior of the package has not been exposed to air. Once exposed to air, beef will change from dark red to bright red. With extended exposure to air, beef will turn from red in color to brown in color. Color changes are normal, so you should use the "sell by" date on the package as a guide.

Storing Ground Beef:

- For future use, freeze cooked and/or seasoned ground beef in portions. It should be frozen immediately after being cooked and used within three months.
- If well wrapped, uncooked ground beef can be frozen for two to three months. Fresh ground beef will keep for two to three days in the refrigerator.
- To keep uncooked hamburger patties from sticking together when freezing, separate each with a square of wax paper or plastic wrap.

Cooking with Ground Beef:

- Ground beef should be cooked to an interior temperature of 160° in order to kill bacteria.*
- Wash your hands before and after you handle raw ground beef.

- Ground beef should always be defrosted in the refrigerator or microwave and never at room temperature.
- To avoid cross contamination, once raw meat is transferred to the grill, broiler or another baking dish, wash the original plate it was resting on before placing the meat back on it, or use a different clean plate.
- Frozen hamburger patties should not be cooked until after they are completely thawed. A partially or completely frozen patty will not cook evenly. While the sides may look done, the center may not be completely cooked.
- Dishes such as meatloaf should be checked with a meat thermometer to ensure doneness, especially if the beef is being cooked with dark sauces that could hide the actual color of the meat.
- Wet hands with water when forming meatballs to keep the ground beef from sticking to your hands.
- To form uniform-size meatballs, form ground beef mixture into a 1" thick rectangle on a sheet of wax paper. Cut the ground beef into even 1" cubes and roll the cubes into meatballs.

* According to the United States Department of Agriculture, bacteria are everywhere in our environment and any food of animal origin can harbor bacteria such as Salmonella or E. coli.

These bacteria can multiply rapidly between the temperatures of 40° to 140° F. To keep these levels low, meat should be stored in the refrigerator at 40° or less. To destroy the bacteria, meat should be cooked to 160° F.

Bacteria can also spread from one surface to another. Juices from meat can contaminate other foods that are safe or have been cooked safely. To avoid this, wash your hands before and after you handle raw meat and do not reuse any containers, utensils or surfaces that have come into contact with raw meat without washing them first.

Reducing Fat in Cooked Ground Beef:

According to the National Cattlemen's Beef Association, a simple rinsing process will reduce the fat content of cooked beef crumbles by almost 50 percent. This technique allows you to take advantage of lower-priced, higher-fat ground beef with the benefit of a leaner product and very little loss of flavor.

To reduce the fat, cook and crumble ground beef in a medium skillet over medium-high heat for 8 to 10 minutes or until browned; drain grease from skillet. In a microwave-safe bowl, warm 4 cups of water on high for 5 to 6 minutes or until very hot, but not boiling. Using a slotted spoon, transfer cooked beef to a plate lined with three paper towels. Let sit for 1 minute and blot top of beef with another paper towel. Place beef in a colander and pour hot water over the beef to rinse the fat off. Let drain for 5 minutes. If a recipe calls for ground beef to be browned with vegetables, these foods can be included in the rinsing process.

BEEFED UP

Soups and Stews

Beef and Potato Soup

1 lb. ground beef
1 medium onion, chopped
1 (16 oz.) can whole peeled tomatoes, in liquid
6 potatoes, peeled and cubed
1 (8 oz.) can tomato sauce
3 C. water
2 tsp. salt
1 tsp. pepper
1 tsp. hot pepper sauce

In a medium skillet over medium-high heat, cook ground beef and onion until beef is browned and onion is tender. Drain the grease from the skillet. In a large saucepan, combine the beef and onion mixture, tomatoes and liquid, potatoes and tomato sauce. Stir in the water, salt, pepper and hot pepper sauce; bring to a boil. Reduce heat and cover. Let the soup simmer for 45 minutes or until potatoes are tender.

Hamburger Veggie Soup

Makes 5 servings

1 lb. ground beef
1 medium onion, chopped
1 C. uncooked elbow macaroni
3 (14 oz.) cans beef broth
2 (14.5 oz.) cans stewed tomatoes, in liquid
1 (16 oz.) pkg. frozen peas, thawed
1 tsp. pepper
1 tsp. garlic salt

In a large stock pot over medium-high heat, cook ground beef and chopped onion until beef is browned and onion is tender. Drain the grease from the pot. Bring a large pot of lightly salted water to a boil. Add elbow macaroni and cook for 8 to 10 minutes or until macaroni is tender. Drain water from pot and add the macaroni, beef broth, stewed tomatoes and liquid, frozen peas, pepper and garlic salt to the ground beef in the stock pot. Cook soup over medium heat for 15 minutes or until peas are cooked. Let the soup simmer until ready to be served.

Excellent Eggplant Stew

Makes 8 servings

1 T. vegetable oil
1 medium onion, chopped
1 lb. ground beef
1 clove garlic, crushed
1 medium eggplant, diced
¾ C. sliced carrots
¾ C. sliced celery
2 (14.5 oz.) cans Italian diced tomatoes, drained
2 (14 oz.) cans beef broth
1 tsp. sugar
½ tsp. ground nutmeg
1 tsp. salt
½ tsp. pepper
½ C. uncooked elbow macaroni
2 tsp. chopped fresh parsley
½ C. grated Parmesan cheese

In a medium skillet over medium heat, heat the vegetable oil. Add the chopped onion, ground beef and crushed garlic; cook until beef is browned and vegetables are tender. Drain the grease from the skillet and mix in the diced eggplant, sliced carrots, sliced celery and Italian diced tomatoes. Pour in the beef broth. Mix in the sugar and season with nutmeg, salt and pepper. Cook and stir the mixture until heated through. Add the uncooked macaroni to the soup and cook for 12 minutes more or until macaroni is al dente. Stir in chopped fresh parsley. Ladle the soup into separate serving bowls and sprinkle with Parmesan cheese before serving.

Two-Meat Italian Soup

Makes 8 servings

1 lb. ground beef
1 lb. ground pork sausage
1 C. chopped onion
2 cloves garlic, minced
1 C. chopped green pepper
2 C. Italian green beans
3½ C. diced zucchini
1 (29 oz.) can tomato sauce
1 (14.5 oz.) can diced tomatoes, drained
1½ T. Italian-style seasoning
1 tsp. salt
½ tsp. pepper
¼ C. grated Parmesan cheese

In a large skillet over medium-high heat, cook ground beef, ground pork sausage, chopped onion, minced garlic and chopped green pepper for 15 minutes or until the meat is browned and vegetables are tender. Drain the grease from the skillet and transfer the meat and vegetable mixture to a stock pot. Add Italian green beans, diced zucchini, tomato sauce and diced tomatoes. Season the soup with Italian-style seasoning, salt and pepper. Bring the soup to a boil, then reduce heat and let simmer for 30 minutes. Ladle the soup into separate serving bowls and sprinkle with Parmesan cheese before serving.

Super Spaghetti Soup

Makes 6 servings

1 lb. ground beef
1 C. chopped onion
1 clove garlic, minced
2 (14.5 oz.) cans diced tomatoes, in liquid
1 (15.25 oz.) can whole kernel corn, in liquid
8 C. water
8 oz. uncooked spaghetti

In a large stock pot over medium-high heat, cook ground beef for 5 to 10 minutes or until meat is thoroughly browned. Add the chopped onion and minced garlic and cook for 2 minutes more. Add the diced tomatoes and liquid, whole kernel corn and liquid and water; bring to a boil and add the uncooked spaghetti. Reduce heat to medium-low and simmer for 15 minutes or until spaghetti is tender.

Slow-Cooked Cheesy Vegetable Soup

Makes 5 servings

1 lb. ground beef
1 (10 oz.) pkg. frozen corn
1 C. cubed potatoes
1 C. sliced celery
1 C. sliced carrots
½ C. chopped onion
2 C. water
2 beef bouillon cubes
¾ tsp. hot pepper sauce
1 (16 oz.) jar processed cheese

In a medium skillet over medium-high heat, cook ground beef until browned. Drain the grease from the skillet. In a slow cooker, place the ground beef, frozen corn, cubed potatoes, sliced celery, sliced carrots, chopped onion, water, beef bouillon cubes and hot pepper sauce. Cook on low for 8 to 10 hours. Add processed cheese during the last 30 minutes of cooking time and stir until well blended and warmed through.

Meaty Corn Chowder

Makes 12 servings

1 lb. ground beef
1 medium onion, chopped
5 medium potatoes, cubed
1 (15 oz.) can creamed corn
1 (15.25 oz.) can whole kernel corn, in liquid
2 C. milk

In a medium skillet over medium-high heat, cook ground beef and chopped onion until meat is browned and onion is tender. Drain the grease from the skillet. In a large stock pot with as little water as possible, cook cubed potatoes for 20 minutes or until tender. Add creamed corn, whole kernel corn and liquid, milk and beef mixture to the potatoes and simmer for 30 minutes.

Lasagna Soup

1 lb. ground beef
5 C. water
1 (14.5 oz.) can diced tomatoes, drained
1½ C. quartered fresh mushrooms
¾ C. chopped green pepper
½ C. diced onion
1 clove garlic, minced
1 tsp. dried basil
Salt and pepper to taste
¾ C. crumbled feta cheese

In a large stock pot over medium heat, cook ground beef until browned. Drain the grease from the stock pot. Add the water, diced tomatoes, quartered mushrooms, chopped green pepper, diced onion and minced garlic to the ground beef, mixing well. Season the mixture with basil, salt and pepper. Bring to a boil, then reduce heat and simmer for 45 minutes. Mix the crumbled feta cheese into the soup and cook for 15 minutes more.

Herbed Chili

Makes 4 servings

1 lb. ground beef
2½ T. flour
1 (16 oz.) can Italian-style tomatoes, in liquid
1 (15.25 oz.) can dark red kidney beans, drained
2 C. chopped onion
⅓ C. tomato paste
⅓ C. water
1½ to 2 T. chili powder
1 T. dried parsley
2 tsp. dried dillweed
1½ tsp. crushed dried oregano
1¼ tsp. crushed dried basil
1 tsp. pepper
½ tsp. salt
Chopped onion, optional
Sour cream, optional
Shredded Cheddar cheese, optional

In a large stock pot over medium-high heat, cook ground beef until browned. Drain the grease from the pot. Stir in flour and add tomatoes and liquid, kidney beans, chopped onion, tomato paste, water, chili powder, dried parsley, dried dillweed, crushed dried oregano, crushed dried basil, pepper and salt. Bring the mixture to a boil. Reduce heat, cover and simmer for 20 minutes, stirring occasionally. To serve, ladle chili into warm soup bowls and top with additional chopped onion, sour cream and shredded Cheddar cheese, if desired.

Beef and Baked Beans Stew

Makes 4 to 6 servings

1 lb. ground beef
½ C. chopped onion
½ C. chopped green bell pepper
½ C. shredded carrots
1 (8 oz.) can tomato sauce
1 C. water
½ tsp. garlic powder
1 (28 oz.) can baked beans
1 (14.5 oz.) can diced tomatoes, in liquid
1 C. shredded Cheddar cheese

In large skillet over medium-high heat, cook ground beef, chopped onion and green bell pepper until beef is browned and vegetables are tender. Drain the grease from the skillet. In a large stock pot over medium-low heat, combine the beef mixture, shredded carrots, tomato sauce, water, garlic powder, baked beans and diced tomatoes and liquid. Cover and simmer for 45 minutes to 1 hour. To serve, spoon the stew into bowls and sprinkle with shredded Cheddar cheese.

Fuss-Free Chili

Makes 4 servings

1 lb. ground beef
1 onion, chopped
1 (14.5 oz.) can stewed tomatoes, in liquid
1 (15 oz.) can tomato sauce
1 (15 oz.) can kidney beans
1½ C. water
Pinch of chili powder
Pinch of garlic powder
Salt and pepper to taste

In a large saucepan over medium-high heat, cook ground beef and chopped onion until beef is browned and onion is tender. Drain the grease from the saucepan. Add the stewed tomatoes and liquid, tomato sauce, kidney beans and water. Season the soup with the chili powder, garlic powder, salt and pepper. Bring the soup to a boil, then reduce heat to low, cover and let simmer for 15 minutes.

Slow-Cooked Cabbage Beef Stew

Makes 4 servings

1 lb. ground beef
1 onion, chopped
1 (15 oz.) can ranch-style beans
¼ tsp. ground cumin
3 cloves garlic, minced
2½ C. chopped cabbage
1 green bell pepper, chopped
1 (14.5 oz.) can stewed tomatoes, in liquid
2 stalks celery, chopped
¼ C. picante sauce
1 C. water
Salt and pepper to taste

In a medium skillet over medium-high heat, cook ground beef and onion until the meat is browned and onion is tender. Drain the grease from the skillet. Combine the ranch-style beans, ground cumin, minced garlic, chopped cabbage and chopped green bell pepper in a slow cooker. Stir in stewed tomatoes and liquid, chopped celery, picante sauce, water and beef mixture. Season the stew with salt and pepper. Cover and cook on low for 6 to 8 hours.

Beanless But Beefy Chili

Makes 6 servings

1 lb. ground beef
2 cloves garlic, minced
1 large onion, chopped
2 T. chili powder
1 tsp. dried oregano
1 tsp. ground cumin
1 tsp. hot pepper sauce
1 (28 oz.) can crushed tomatoes, in liquid
¼ C. red wine vinegar

In a large stock pot over medium-high heat, cook the ground beef, minced garlic and chopped onion until beef is browned and vegetables are tender. Drain the grease from the skillet. Season the ground beef mixture with chili powder, dried oregano, ground cumin and hot pepper sauce. Stir in the crushed tomatoes and liquid and red wine vinegar. Bring the soup to a boil, then reduce heat to low and simmer for about 1 hour, stirring occasionally.

BEEFED UP

Burgers and Sandwiches

Pepperoni Sausage Burgers

1 lb. ground beef
¼ lb. pepperoni sausage, minced
¼ C. dry Italian seasoned bread crumbs
1 clove garlic, minced
Salt and pepper to taste
6 hamburger buns

Preheat the grill to medium-high heat. Brush the grill grate with oil. In a medium bowl, mix the ground beef, pepperoni sausage, Italian seasoned bread crumbs, minced garlic, salt and pepper. Form the mixture into six hamburger patties. Place the hamburger patties on the grill. Cook the patties for 5 to 7 minutes on each side or to desired doneness. To serve, place each hamburger patty on a bun.

Rockin' Wasabi Burgers

Makes 4 servings

1 lb. ground beef
¼ C. minced onion
2 cloves garlic, minced
Salt and pepper to taste
4 hamburger buns
4 T. wasabi paste
4 T. mayonnaise
4 hamburger buns
4 slices Cheddar cheese

Preheat the grill to medium-high heat. Brush the grill grate with oil. In a large bowl, mix the ground beef, minced onion and minced garlic. Season the mixture with salt and pepper; shape into four hamburger patties. Place the hamburger patties on the grill. Cook the patties for 5 to 7 minutes on each side or to desired doneness. Brush the bottom of each hamburger bun with 1 tablespoon of wasabi paste. Brush the top of each hamburger bun with 1 tablespoon of mayonnaise. Top each hamburger patty with a slice of Cheddar cheese and place on a prepared bun to serve.

Mouthwatering Loose Meat Sandwiches

Makes 4 servings

1 lb. ground beef
1 T. mayonnaise
1 T. vinegar
1 T. sugar
1 T. mustard
1 T. Worcestershire sauce
Ketchup to taste
4 hamburger buns

In a medium skillet over medium-high heat, cook ground beef until browned. Drain the grease from the skillet. Add the mayonnaise, vinegar, sugar, mustard, Worcestershire sauce and ketchup to ground beef. Let the beef mixture simmer over low heat for 15 to 20 minutes or until heated through. Spoon the mixture onto the hamburger buns to serve.

Beefy BBQ Sandwiches

Makes 4 to 6 servings

1 lb. ground beef
1 small onion, diced
½ C. diced celery
¾ C. ketchup
¼ C. smoked barbecue sauce
1 tsp. dry mustard
1 T. vinegar
¼ C. brown sugar
4 to 6 hamburger buns

In a medium skillet over medium-high heat, cook ground beef, diced onion and diced celery until the beef is browned and the vegetables are tender. Drain the grease from the skillet. Add the ketchup, smoked barbecue sauce, dry mustard, vinegar and brown sugar to the beef mixture. Let the mixture simmer over low heat for 15 to 20 minutes or until heated through. Spoon the beef mixture onto the hamburger buns to serve.

Mexican Meatball Sandwiches

1 C. picante sauce, divided
1 lb. ground beef
1 C. crushed tortilla chips
1 egg, beaten
1 tsp. dried parsley
1½ C. spaghetti sauce
6 long hard rolls, split

In a large bowl, mix ½ cup picante sauce, ground beef, crushed tortilla chips, egg and dried parsley. Shape the mixture into 18 meatballs about 1½" diameter each. In a medium skillet over medium heat, mix the spaghetti sauce and remaining ½ cup picante sauce. Add meatballs to the sauce mixture and bring to a boil. Reduce the heat to low and cook, stirring occasionally, for 20 minutes or until the meatballs are no longer pink. To serve, place three meatballs on each roll.

Pineapple Salsa Jerk Burgers

Makes 4 servings

2 tsp. vegetable oil
1 C. minced green bell peppers
¼ C. minced red bell peppers
¼ C. minced onion
1 tsp. minced gingerroot
1 (8 oz.) can crushed pineapple, drained
¼ C. apple jelly
1 T. lime juice
Pinch of salt
1 lb. ground beef
3 T. jerk sauce, divided
4 hamburger buns
1 C. shredded Monterey Jack cheese

Preheat the grill to medium-high heat. Brush the grill grate with oil. In a medium saucepan over medium heat, heat oil. Add minced green bell peppers, minced red bell peppers, minced onion and minced gingerroot to the oil; cook for 3 minutes. Add crushed pineapple, apple jelly, lime juice and salt; cook until the jelly melts, then set pineapple salsa aside. In a medium bowl, mix together the ground beef and 1 tablespoon jerk sauce. Shape beef into four hamburger patties. Brush both sides of the hamburger patties with the remaining jerk sauce. Cook the patties on the grill for 5 to 7 minutes on each side or to desired doneness. Split hamburger buns and place ¼ cup of Monterey Jack cheese on the bottom half of each bun. Place a hamburger on each bun and top with pineapple salsa. Place the top of bun over salsa and serve.

Beef Calzones

Makes 4 servings

2 T. cornmeal
2 T. plus 1 tsp. olive oil, divided
½ C. minced onion
¼ C. chopped celery
1 T. minced garlic
¼ tsp. salt
1 lb. ground beef
1 (24 oz.) jar marinara sauce
¼ C. chopped carrot
1 (13.5 oz.) tube refrigerated pizza dough
4 T. grated Parmesan cheese

Preheat the oven to 425° and place the oven rack on the lowest level. Sprinkle the cornmeal over a baking sheet and set aside. In a large skillet over medium heat, heat 1 teaspoon olive oil. Add the minced onion, chopped celery, minced garlic and salt; cook and stir for 3 minutes or until vegetables are soft. Stir in the ground beef and cook 3 to 5 minutes or until ground beef is no longer pink. Add marinara sauce and chopped carrot. Reduce heat to medium-low and simmer, uncovered, for 15 minutes. Transfer the mixture to a large bowl and let cool for 15 to 20 minutes. Divide the refrigerated pizza dough into four pieces. Lightly roll each piece in flour and shape into a 7" circle. Spread ½ cup of the meat filling onto half of each dough circle, leaving a ½" border. Sprinkle 1 tablespoon of Parmesan cheese over the meat filling of each calzone. Fold half of the dough over the meat and seal the dough edges together. Transfer the calzones to the prepared baking sheet. Brush the top of each calzone with ½ tablespoon of olive oil. Bake for 15 to 20 minutes or until golden brown.

Meatball Pitas

Makes 8 servings

½ C. plain yogurt
1 tsp. lemon juice
1 tsp. minced garlic, divided
¼ tsp. salt
1 lb. ground beef
1 T. chopped fresh oregano
¾ tsp. salt
¼ tsp. ground red pepper
2 tsp. olive oil
2 T. water
4 pita bread rounds, cut in half
8 lettuce leaves
Tomato wedges, optional

In a small bowl, combine plain yogurt, lemon juice, ½ teaspoon minced garlic and salt; set aside. In a medium bowl, combine the ground beef, chopped fresh oregano, salt, remaining ½ teaspoon minced garlic and ground red pepper. Form 16 meatballs about ½" in diameter and place on a sheet of wax paper. In a large skillet over medium-high heat, heat the olive oil. Add the meatballs and cook 4 to 6 minutes or until browned on all sides. Using a paper towel, soak up the grease in the bottom of the skillet and discard. Reduce heat to medium and add water. Cover and cook 2 to 3 minutes more or until meatballs are cooked through. To serve, place 2 meatballs in each pita half and top with 1 tablespoon of the yogurt sauce, 1 lettuce leaf and tomato wedges.

Tasty Taco Burgers

1 (0.9 oz.) env. onion and mushroom soup mix
1 lb. ground beef
½ C. chopped tomato
¼ C. chopped bell pepper
1 tsp. chili powder
¼ C. water
4 hamburger buns
Shredded lettuce, optional
Shredded Cheddar cheese, optional

Preheat the grill to medium-high heat. Brush the grill grate with oil. In a large bowl, combine the onion and mushroom soup mix, ground beef, chopped tomato, chopped green bell pepper, chili powder and water; shape into four hamburger patties. Grill hamburger patties for 5 to 7 minutes on each side or to desired doneness. Place one hamburger on each bun and, if desired, top with shredded lettuce and cheese to serve.

Cheese Stuffed Surprise Burgers

Makes 4 servings

½ (0.9 oz.) env. onion soup mix
1 lb. ground beef
¼ C. water
¾ C. shredded Cheddar, mozzarella
   or Monterey Jack cheese, divided
4 hamburger buns

Preheat the grill to medium-high heat. Brush the grill grate with oil. In a large bowl, combine the onion soup mix, ground beef and water. Shape the mixture into eight thin hamburger patties. Place 2 tablespoons of cheese in the center of four of the hamburger patties. Place remaining four hamburger patties on top of the ones with cheese and seal the edges of the two patties tightly. Grill for 5 to 7 minutes on each side or to desired doneness. To serve, place each hamburger patty on a bun.

Super Stuffed French Bread

Makes 4 to 6 servings

1 lb. ground beef
1 medium onion, chopped
3 cloves garlic, minced
¼ C. chopped fresh parsley
1 loaf French bread
1 (10.75 oz.) can cream of mushroom soup
Salt and pepper to taste
1½ C. shredded Cheddar, mozzarella
   or Monterey Jack cheese

Preheat the oven to 350°. In a large skillet over medium-high heat, cook the ground beef, chopped onion, minced garlic and chopped fresh parsley. Cook until ground beef is browned and vegetables are tender. Drain the grease from the skillet. Carve out the top of the French bread loaf leaving a cap that will be replaced later. Hollow out the inside of the loaf. Break apart bread pieces and place in a medium bowl. Add the hamburger mixture, cream of mushroom soup, salt and pepper. Mix well and stuff into the hollowed French bread loaf. Sprinkle the shredded Cheddar, mozzarella or Monterey Jack cheese over top and place the cap back on the loaf of bread. Wrap the stuffed French bread in foil and bake in the oven for 20 minutes. To serve, slice the stuffed French bread into 4 to 6 pieces.

West Coast Burgers

Makes 4 servings

1 lb. ground beef
1½ C. chopped onion
1½ C. chopped celery
1 T. mustard
3 T. vinegar
1 (10.75 oz.) can tomato soup
1 T. sugar
Salt and pepper, to taste
4 hamburger buns

In a large skillet over medium-high heat, cook ground beef, chopped onion and chopped celery. Cook until ground beef is browned and vegetables are tender. Add mustard, vinegar, tomato soup, sugar, salt and pepper. Simmer for 30 minutes or until heated through. To serve, spoon the ground beef mixture on each of the hamburger buns.

Corny Cumin Burgers

1 lb. ground beef
1 T. ground cumin
1 T. cumin seeds
1 C. canned whole kernel corn, drained
Salt and pepper to taste
4 hamburger buns

Preheat the grill to medium-high heat. Brush the grill grate with oil. In a large bowl, combine ground beef, ground cumin, cumin seeds, corn, salt and pepper. Form the beef mixture into four hamburger patties. Brush the grill grate with oil and place the burger patties on the grill. Cook hamburger patties for 5 to 7 minutes on each side or to desired doneness. To serve, place each patty on a hamburger bun.

Buffalo Burgers

Makes 4 servings

1 lb. ground beef
1 (10.75 oz.) can tomato soup
⅛ tsp. hot pepper sauce
4 hamburger buns, toasted*
½ C. crumbled blue cheese

Shape the ground beef into four hamburger patties. In a medium skillet over medium-high heat, cook the hamburger patties until browned on both sides. Remove patties from skillet and set aside. Drain the grease from the skillet. Add tomato soup and hot pepper sauce to the skillet; heat to a boil. Return hamburger patties to skillet and reduce heat to low. Cover and cook for 10 minutes or until patties are no longer pink. To serve, place each patty on a hamburger bun and sprinkle the patty with crumbled blue cheese.

* To toast, split hamburger buns and place in a single layer on a baking sheet. Bake in the oven at 350° for 5 minutes or until buns are slightly crisp and golden.

Blue Burgers

2 T. olive oil

2 T. red wine vinegar

1 tsp. chopped fresh thyme

¾ tsp. pepper, divided

2 medium yellow squash, cut lengthwise in ½" thick pieces

1 lb. ground beef

½ tsp. salt

4 hamburger buns

2 to 4 oz. blue cheese

Arugula or lettuce, optional

Preheat the grill to medium-high heat. Brush the grill grate with oil. In a medium bowl, whisk together olive oil, red wine vinegar, chopped fresh thyme and ¼ teaspoon pepper. Brush the squash pieces with the dressing. Set aside remaining dressing. In a medium bowl, combine the ground beef, salt and remaining ½ teaspoon pepper. Shape the ground beef into four hamburger patties. Cook hamburger patties on the grill for 5 to 7 minutes on each side or to desired doneness. Cook the squash directly on the grill next to the hamburger patties for 7 to 10 minutes or until tender. To serve, drizzle leftover dressing on the top half of each bun. Place one hamburger patty on each bun, top with squash, blue cheese and, if desired, arugula or lettuce.

Fabulous French Onion Burgers

Makes 4 servings

1 lb. ground beef
1 (10.5 oz.) can French onion soup
4 round hard rolls, split
4 slices cheese, any kind

Shape the ground beef into four hamburger patties. In a medium skillet over medium-high heat, cook the hamburger patties until browned on both sides. Set the hamburger patties aside. Drain the grease from the skillet. Add the French onion soup to the skillet and heat to a boil. Return the hamburger patties to the pan and reduce heat to low. Cover and cook for 5 to 7 minutes on each side or to desired doneness. To serve, place each patty on one round hard roll and top with one slice of cheese. Use leftover French onion soup as dipping sauce.

Sloppy Taco Joes

1 lb. ground beef
1 (16 oz.) can whole tomatoes, in liquid
1 tsp. Worcestershire sauce
1 to 2 tsp. chili powder
1 tsp. garlic salt
½ tsp. ground mustard
½ tsp. ground cumin
½ tsp. sugar
8 hamburger buns, toasted*
1 C. shredded Cheddar cheese
2 C. shredded lettuce

In a medium skillet over medium-high heat, cook ground beef until browned. Drain the grease from the skillet. Add tomatoes and liquid, Worcestershire sauce, chili powder, garlic salt, ground mustard, ground cumin and sugar. Stir well and bring to a boil. Reduce the heat and simmer, uncovered, for 15 to 20 minutes or until thickened. To serve, spoon ground beef mixture onto toasted buns; top with Cheddar cheese and shredded lettuce.

* To toast, split hamburger buns and place in a single layer on a baking sheet. Bake in the oven at 350° for 5 minutes or until buns are slightly crisp and golden.

Zing-Burgers

1 lb. ground beef
4 tsp. horseradish
2 tsp. Dijon mustard
1 tsp. paprika
¼ tsp. pepper
⅛ tsp. salt, optional
4 hamburger buns

Preheat the grill to medium-high heat. Brush the grill grate with oil. In a medium bowl, combine the ground beef, horseradish, Dijon mustard, paprika, pepper and salt. Shape the mixture into four hamburger patties. Cook hamburger patties on the grill for 5 to 7 minutes on each side or to desired doneness. To serve, place each hamburger patty on a bun.

Meatball Baguette Sandwiches

Makes 4 servings

1 lb. ground beef
¾ C. bread crumbs
2 tsp. dried Italian seasoning
2 cloves garlic, minced
2 T. chopped fresh parsley
2 T. grated Parmesan cheese
1 egg, beaten
1 French baguette
1 T. extra-virgin olive oil
½ tsp. garlic powder
Pinch of salt
1 (14 oz.) jar spaghetti sauce
4 slices provolone cheese

Preheat the oven to 350°. In a medium bowl, mix together ground beef, bread crumbs, Italian seasoning, minced garlic, chopped fresh parsley, Parmesan cheese and egg. Shape the mixture into 12 meatballs and place in a 9 x 13" baking dish. Bake in the oven for 15 to 20 minutes or until cooked through. Cut the French baguette in half lengthwise and slightly hollow out the inside to make a well for the meatballs. Brush both cut sides of the baguette with olive oil and season with garlic powder and salt. Toast both halves of the baguette in the preheated oven next to the meatballs for 5 minutes or until slightly crisp and golden. In a medium saucepan over medium heat, warm the spaghetti sauce. Remove the meatballs from the oven and combine with spaghetti sauce. Spoon the meatballs and sauce into the baguette and top with slices of provolone cheese. Return the baguette to the oven and bake for 2 to 3 minutes or until the cheese has melted. To serve, cut the baguette into 4 portions.

Saucy All-American Burgers

1 clove garlic, minced or 2 T. minced onion
2 T. ketchup
1 T. steak sauce
1 T. Worcestershire sauce
1 tsp. sugar
1 tsp. vegetable oil
1 tsp. vinegar
2 to 3 dashes hot pepper sauce
1 lb. ground beef
¼ tsp. salt
¼ tsp. pepper
4 hamburger buns, toasted*

Preheat the grill to medium-high heat. Brush the grill grate with oil. In a small saucepan over medium-high heat, combine minced garlic or minced onion, ketchup, steak sauce, Worcestershire sauce, sugar, vegetable oil, vinegar and hot pepper sauce; bring to a boil. Reduce heat and let simmer, uncovered, for 5 minutes. Remove from heat and set aside. In medium bowl, mix together ground beef, salt and pepper. Shape the ground beef into four hamburger patties. Cook hamburger patties on the grill for 5 to 7 minutes on each side or to desired doneness. While cooking, brush the burgers frequently with sauce. To serve, place one hamburger patty on each bun.

*To toast, split hamburger buns and place in a single layer on a baking sheet. Bake in the oven at 350° for 5 minutes or until buns are slightly crisp and golden.

Sizzling Cilantro Burgers

Makes 4 servings

1 lb. ground beef
1 C. barbecue sauce
1 tsp. garlic powder
4 slices Monterey Jack cheese
1 C. chopped fresh cilantro, divided
8 slices sourdough bread, toasted*
4 lettuce leaves
4 slices tomato

Preheat the grill to medium-high heat. Brush the grill grate with oil. In a medium bowl, mix together ground beef, barbecue sauce and garlic powder. Shape the mixture into four hamburger patties. Cook the hamburger patties on the grill for 5 to 7 minutes on each side or to desired doneness. Place a slice of Monterey Jack cheese on each burger and let melt for 1 minute. Press ¼ cup of chopped fresh cilantro onto each slice of melted cheese. To serve, place each burger on a slice of sour dough bread and top with lettuce, tomato and another slice of bread.

*To toast, place slices of bread in a single layer on a baking sheet. Bake in the oven at 350° for 5 minutes or until bread slices are slightly crisp and golden.

Two-Pepper Burgers

Makes 4 servings

1 egg, beaten
¼ C. dry bread crumbs
6 slices bacon, cooked and crumbled
2 to 3 jalepeno peppers, seeded and finely chopped
2 T. milk
1 lb. ground beef
1 green bell pepper, seeded and cut into rings
1 small onion, thinly sliced and separated into rings
2 T. butter
4 hamburger buns, toasted*

Preheat the grill to medium-high heat. In a large bowl, stir together egg, dry bread crumbs, crumbled bacon, chopped jalepeno peppers and milk. Add in ground beef and shape mixture into four hamburger patties. Cook the hamburger patties on the grill for 5 to 7 minutes on each side or to desired doneness. In a small saucepan over medium-high heat, cook the green pepper rings and sliced onion in butter until tender. To serve, place each hamburger patty on a bun and top with pepper and onion mixture.

*To toast, split hamburger buns and place in a single layer on a baking sheet. Bake in the oven at 350° for 5 minutes or until buns are slightly crisp and golden.

Grilled Gyro Burgers

Makes 4 servings

1⅓ (8 oz.) containers plain yogurt, divided
⅔ (1 oz.) env. ranch dressing mix
1 small cucumber, peeled, seeded and chopped
1 lb. ground beef
2½ T. diced onion
4 pita bread rounds
1⅓ cups torn lettuce leaves
1 small tomato, seeded and diced

Preheat the grill to medium-high heat and brush the grill grate with oil. In a medium bowl, combine half the plain yogurt and the ranch dressing mix. Remove half of the mixture and place in a separate bowl. Into one of the bowls, mix in the remaining half of the plain yogurt and the diced cucumber. Cover the cucumber and yogurt mixture and refrigerate. Mix the ground beef and the diced onion into the remaining ranch and yogurt mixture. Shape the beef mixture into four hamburger patties. Cook hamburger patties on the grill for 5 to 7 minutes on each side or to desired doneness. Cut off ¼ of the end of each pita pocket to create an opening in the pocket. Fill with torn lettuce and 1 hamburger patty. To serve, top with cucumber-yogurt sauce and diced tomato.

Rosemary Burgers

Makes 4 servings

1 lb. ground beef
½ tsp. crushed dried rosemary
Pinch salt
Pinch pepper
¼ tsp. garlic powder
4 T. butter
4 hamburger buns

Preheat the grill to medium-high heat. Brush the grill grate with oil. In a medium bowl, mix together ground beef, crushed dried rosemary, salt, pepper and garlic powder. Shape the mixture into four balls. Make an indentation in the center of each ball and place 1 tablespoon of butter in each hole. Mold the ground beef around the hole and flatten each ball into a hamburger patty. Cook the hamburger patties on the grill for 5 to 7 minutes on each side or to desired doneness. To serve, place each patty on a hamburger bun.

Pineapple Hide and Seek Burgers

Makes 4 servings

1 lb. ground beef
4 pineapple rings
½ C. ketchup
½ C. brown sugar
1 T. mustard
4 hamburger buns, optional

Preheat the grill to medium-high heat. Shape the ground beef into eight thin hamburger patties. Place one pineapple ring on four of the hamburger patties. Place the remaining four hamburger patties on top of each pineapple ring and seal the edges of the two patties around the pineapple rings. In a small saucepan over medium-high heat, mix the ketchup, brown sugar and mustard; heat until the sugar is dissolved and set aside. Cook the hamburger patties on the grill for 5 to 7 minutes on each side or to desired doneness. To serve, spoon the ketchup and brown sugar sauce over each hamburger and place on a bun if desired.

Southern Seasoned Burgers

1 lb. ground beef
½ small onion, finely chopped
6 T. brown sugar
1 tsp. Cajun seasoning
1 tsp. garlic powder
2 T. steak sauce
¼ C. Italian seasoned bread crumbs
4 hamburger buns

Preheat the grill to medium-high heat. Brush the grill grate with oil. In a medium bowl, mix together ground beef, chopped onion, brown sugar, Cajun seasoning, garlic powder, steak sauce and bread crumbs. Shape the mixture into four hamburger patties. Cook the hamburger patties on the grill for 5 to 7 minutes on each side or to desired doneness. To serve, place each patty on a hamburger bun.

Sensational Sour Cream Burgers

Makes 4 servings

1 lb. ground beef
½ C. sour cream
½ (1 oz.) env. onion soup mix
¼ C. dry bread crumbs
Pinch of pepper
4 hamburger buns

Preheat the grill to medium-high heat. Brush the grill grate with oil. In a medium bowl, mix together ground beef, sour cream, onion soup mix, dry bread crumbs and pepper. Chill in the refrigerator while the grill preheats. Shape the beef mixture into four hamburger patties. Cook hamburger patties on the grill for 5 to 7 minutes on each side or to desired doneness. To serve, place each patty on a hamburger bun.

Firecracker Jack Burgers

1 lb. ground beef
1 (4 oz.) can diced green chilies, drained
1 tsp. beef bouillon granules
4 slices Monterey Jack cheese
4 hamburger buns

Preheat the grill to medium-high heat. Brush the grill grate with oil. In a medium bowl, mix together ground beef, diced green chilies and beef bouillon granules. Shape the mixture into four hamburger patties. Cook the hamburger patties on the grill for 5 to 7 minutes on each side or to desired doneness. Top each patty with a slice of cheese 2 minutes prior to removing from the grill. To serve, place each patty on a hamburger bun.

Sweet Brown Sugar Burgers

Makes 4 servings

⅓ C. plus 1 T. Worcestershire Sauce
⅓ C. plus 1 T. brown sugar
½ tsp. garlic powder
½ tsp. seasoned salt
¼ tsp. celery seed
¼ tsp. Italian seasoning
¼ tsp. chopped fresh basil
1 lb. ground beef
¼ medium onion, diced
Salt and pepper to taste
4 hamburger buns

Preheat the grill to medium-high heat. Brush the grill grate with oil. In a medium saucepan over medium-high heat, mix the Worcestershire sauce, brown sugar, garlic powder, seasoned salt, celery seed, Italian seasoning and chopped fresh basil. Stir constantly and bring to a boil; cook for 1 minute. In a large bowl, mix the brown sugar sauce, ground beef and diced onion. Form the mixture into four hamburger patties. Cook the hamburger patties on the grill for 5 to 7 minutes on each side or to desired doneness. To serve, season with salt and pepper and place each patty on a hamburger bun.

Strange and Scrumptious Burgers

Makes 4 servings

1 lb. ground beef
2 T. butter
1 large onion, sliced
4 eggs
4 slices Canadian bacon
4 pineapple rings
4 slices Cheddar cheese
1 (8.25 oz.) can sliced beets, drained
4 slices tomato
4 lettuce leaves
4 Kaiser rolls, split

Preheat the grill to medium-high heat. Brush the grill grate with oil. Form the ground beef into four hamburger patties. Cook the hamburger patties on the grill for 5 to 7 minutes on each side. In a medium skillet over medium-high heat, melt butter. Add onions to butter and cook until tender; remove from the skillet. Crack the eggs, keeping separated, into the same skillet and cook until yolks are solid, turning once. Remove eggs and set aside. Place the Canadian bacon in the same skillet and cook until slightly crisp on the edges. Remove the bacon and set aside. Increase the heat to high and place the pineapple rings in the same skillet. Cook pineapple rings until browned on each side. To serve, place each hamburger patty on a Kaiser roll. Top with a slice of Cheddar cheese, Canadian bacon, one fried egg, fried onions, beet slices, one pineapple ring, tomato slices and lettuce in that order.

Zesty Pretzel Burgers

Makes 4 to 6 servings

1 lb. ground beef
1 C. honey mustard and onion pretzels, finely crushed
¼ C. finely chopped green bell peppers
1 egg, beaten
Salt and pepper to taste
4 to 6 slices Colby cheese
4 to 6 hamburger buns

Preheat the oven to 375°. Lightly grease a baking dish with olive oil. In a medium bowl, mix together ground beef, finely crushed pretzels, finely chopped green bell pepper and egg. Season the mixture with salt and pepper and form into four thick hamburger patties or six smaller hamburger patties. Arrange the patties in the baking dish and bake in the oven for 30 minutes, turning once, or until the internal temperature reaches 165°. Top each patty with a slice of cheese in the last few minutes of baking time. To serve, place each patty on a hamburger bun.

BEEFED UP

Casseroles, Bakes and Pies

Super Stuffed Pepper Casserole

Makes 4 servings

2½ C. herb seasoned stuffing, divided

1 T. butter, melted

1 lb. ground beef

1 medium onion, chopped

1 (14.5 oz) can whole peeled tomatoes, cut up

1 (8 oz.) can whole kernel corn, drained

2 medium green bell peppers,
   cut lengthwise into quarters

Preheat the oven to 400°. In a medium bowl, mix together ¼ cup herbed seasoned stuffing and butter; set aside. In a medium skillet over medium-high heat, cook ground beef and chopped onion until beef is browned and onion is tender. Drain the grease from the skillet. Add tomatoes, corn and remaining herb seasoned stuffing. Arrange the green peppers in a shallow 2-quart baking dish and spoon beef mixture over the peppers. Cover and bake for 25 minutes or until peppers are tender. Sprinkle reserved stuffing mixture over the green peppers and bake for 5 minutes more or until topping is golden. To serve, spoon casserole onto dinner plates.

Chili Burger Casserole

Makes 6 servings

1 C. uncooked elbow macaroni
1 lb. ground beef
1 (10.75 oz.) can tomato soup
1 (10.75 oz.) can chili beef soup
2 C. shredded Monterey Jack cheese

Bring a large pot of lightly salted water to a boil. Add elbow macaroni and cook for 8 to 10 minutes or until tender. Drain water from pot and set aside. In a large skillet over medium-high heat, cook ground beef until browned. Drain the grease from the skillet. Add tomato soup and chili beef soup and let simmer for 15 minutes. Stir in cooked macaroni. Add cheese and let simmer until melted. To serve, spoon the mixture onto dinner plates.

Chinese Rice Casserole

1 C. uncooked rice
3½ C. chicken broth
¼ tsp. salt
1 lb. ground beef
½ C. chopped onion
1 C. chopped celery
1 (8 oz.) can sliced water chestnuts
½ C. sliced black olives
¼ C. soy sauce

Preheat the oven to 350°. In a 2-quart casserole dish, place uncooked rice; pour chicken broth over rice and let stand. In a medium skillet over medium-high heat, cook ground beef, onion and celery until beef is browned and vegetables are tender. Drain the grease from the skillet. In a 2-quart baking dish, combine rice mixture, beef mixture, sliced water chestnuts, sliced olives and soy sauce; mix well. Cover dish and bake in the oven for 1 hour. Remove from oven, uncover, and bake 30 minutes more. To serve, spoon casserole onto dinner plates.

Chow Mein Casserole

Makes 4 to 6 servings

1 lb. ground beef
1 large onion, chopped
1 (15 oz.) can bean sprouts, in liquid
1 C. chopped celery
1 (10.75 oz.) can cream of mushroom soup
1 (5 oz.) can chow mein noodles

Preheat the oven to 350°. In a medium skillet over medium-high heat, cook ground beef and chopped onions until beef is browned and onions are tender. Drain the grease from the skillet. Drain the liquid from the bean sprouts and reserve liquid; set bean sprouts aside. In a medium saucepan over medium-high heat, cook the chopped celery in the bean sprout juice until tender. In a large bowl, mix together cream of mushroom soup, bean sprouts, beef mixture and cooked celery with juice. Place the mixture in a 2-quart baking dish and sprinkle chow mein noodles over the top. Bake in the oven for 1 hour. To serve, spoon mixture onto individual dinner plates.

Cheesy Beef and Potatoes

Makes 4 to 6 servings

1 lb. ground beef
1 medium onion, chopped
1 C. shredded Cheddar cheese
4 to 5 medium potatoes, peeled and thinly sliced
1 (10.75 oz.) can cream of mushroom soup
1 C. water

Preheat the oven to 400°. In a medium skillet over medium-high heat, cook ground beef and chopped onion until ground beef is browned and onion is tender. Drain the grease from the skillet. Place mixture in a greased 9 x 13" baking dish. Sprinkle Cheddar cheese over the top of the beef mixture and place the sliced potatoes over the cheese. In a medium saucepan over medium-high heat, warm cream of mushroom soup and water until heated through. Pour the soup over the sliced potatoes. Bake the casserole for 30 to 45 minutes or until potatoes are tender and golden. To serve, spoon mixture onto dinner plates.

Six Layer Casserole

1 lb. ground beef, divided
2 to 3 potatoes, peeled and sliced
2 to 3 onions, sliced
Salt and pepper to taste
½ C. butter
1 (10.75 oz.) can tomato soup

Preheat the oven to 350°. In a greased 2-quart baking dish, place half the ground beef across the bottom. Top the ground beef with a layer of half of the sliced potatoes. Top the potatoes with a layer of half the sliced onions. Repeat each layer one more time. Salt and pepper the layers to taste. Slice the butter into pieces and place the slices of butter on top of the second layer of the onions. In a medium bowl, mix the tomato soup with a soup can of water. Pour the soup mixture over the casserole. Bake in the oven for 2 hours and 30 minutes. To serve, spoon the casserole onto individual dinner plates.

Microwave Tortilla Casserole

Makes 6 servings

1 lb. ground beef
½ C. chopped onion
½ C. chopped green bell pepper
1 (1.25 oz.) pkg. taco seasoning
1 (8 oz.) can tomato sauce
1 (6 oz.) can tomato paste
½ C. sliced black olives
¼ C. water

½ tsp. chili powder
2 eggs
1 C. sour cream
¼ tsp. pepper
4 flour tortillas
2 C. crushed corn chips
2 C. shredded Monterey Jack cheese

Crumble ground beef, chopped onion and chopped green pepper into a 2-quart microwave-safe dish. Cover and cook in the microwave on high for 5 to 6 minutes or until meat is no longer pink; drain grease from dish. Stir in the taco seasoning, tomato sauce, tomato paste, sliced olives, water and chili powder. Cover and cook at medium power in the microwave for 10 minutes or until thickened, rotating the dish once. In a medium bowl, whisk together eggs, sour cream and pepper. Place two tortillas in the bottom of a 7 x 11" baking dish. Spread a layer of half the sour cream mixture over the tortillas and a layer of half the beef mixture over the sour cream. Repeat each layer beginning with two tortillas. Top the casserole with crushed corn chips and sprinkle Monterey Jack cheese over the chips. Cook in the microwave, uncovered, at medium power for 10 to 15 minutes or until the casserole reaches 160° and the cheese is melted. Let stand for 5 minutes before spooning casserole onto separate dinner plates to serve.

Cheesy Beef and Noodle Casserole

Makes 4 to 6 servings

1 (8 oz.) pkg. dry spiral pasta
1 lb. ground beef
½ green pepper, chopped
½ medium onion, chopped
1 (10.75 oz.) can tomato soup
1 (10.75 oz.) can cream of mushroom soup
1 (10.75 oz.) can Cheddar cheese soup

Preheat the oven to 350°. Bring a large pot of lightly salted water to a boil. Add the spiral pasta and cook for 8 to 10 minutes or until fully cooked. Drain water from pot and set aside. In a medium skillet over medium-high heat, cook ground beef, chopped green pepper and chopped onion until the beef is browned and vegetables are tender. Drain the grease from the skillet. In a large bowl, mix together the tomato soup, cream of mushroom soup and Cheddar cheese soup. Spread the ground beef mixture in the bottom of a 2-quart casserole dish. Pour half of the soup mixture over the beef mixture. Spread the cooked spiral pasta over top of the beef and soup. Pour the remaining soup mixture over the pasta. Bake in the oven for 25 minutes or until heated through. To serve, spoon mixture onto separate dinner plates.

Pasta Pizza Bake

Makes 6 servings

1 (8 oz.) pkg. spiral pasta
1 lb. ground beef
1 small onion, diced
1 (28 oz.) jar spaghetti sauce
4 oz. sliced pepperoni sausage
2 C. shredded mozzarella cheese

Preheat the oven to 350°. Bring a large pot of lightly salted water to a boil. Add the spiral pasta and cook for 8 to 10 minutes or until fully cooked. Drain water from pot and set aside. In a medium skillet over medium-high heat, cook ground beef and diced onion until beef is browned and onion is tender. Drain the grease from the skillet. In a medium bowl, combine the beef mixture, spaghetti sauce, sliced pepperoni and cooked pasta. Pour into a 9 x 13" baking dish and sprinkle mozzarella cheese over the top. Bake in the oven for 30 minutes or until cheese is melted. To serve, spoon mixture onto separate dinner plates.

Greek Patitsio

1 lb. ground beef
1 medium onion, chopped
1 tsp. salt, divided
¼ tsp. pepper, divided
½ C. tomato sauce
¼ tsp. ground cinnamon
3½ C. uncooked elbow
  macaroni

½ C. butter, divided
5 T. flour
3½ C. milk, divided
¾ C. grated Parmesan cheese,
  divided
3 eggs
6 slices thick white bread,
  toasted and cut into cubes

Preheat the oven to 375°. In a large skillet over medium-high heat, cook the ground beef and chopped onion until beef is browned and onion is tender. Drain the grease from the skillet. Stir in ¾ teaspoon salt, ⅛ teaspoon of pepper, tomato sauce and cinnamon; cook 1 to 2 minutes more and set aside. Bring a large pot of lightly salted water to a boil. Add the elbow macaroni and cook for 8 to 10 minutes or until al dente. Drain water from pot and set pasta aside. In a medium saucepan over medium heat, melt ¼ cup butter. Add flour all at once and stir until a smooth roux* is formed. Pour in 2½ cups of milk, a little at a time, and continue to stir until smooth. Stir in ¼ teaspoon salt, ⅛ teaspoon pepper and ¼ cup Parmesan cheese. Bring the mixture to a boil and stir until thickened; remove from heat. In a small bowl, beat together remaining 1 cup milk and eggs; set aside. Place half of the cooked elbow macaroni in a greased 9 x 13" dish and place the beef mixture on top of the pasta. Sprinkle the remaining ½ cup of Parmesan cheese over top. Place the remaining macaroni on top of the cheese. Pour the egg mixture over the macaroni and cover with white sauce. In a medium saucepan over medium heat, melt the remaining ¼ cup of butter. In a medium bowl, stir together the toasted bread cubes and melted butter. Place the bread cubes evenly over the macaroni in the baking dish. Bake in the oven for 50 to 60 minutes or until topping is golden brown. To serve, spoon mixture onto separate dinner plates.

* A roux is a cooked mixture of butter or other fat and flour used to thicken sauces, soups, etc.

Magnificent Mostaccioli Beef Bake

Makes 6 servings

1 (8 oz.) pkg. mostaccioli
1 lb. ground beef
1 medium onion, chopped
1 C. chopped celery
1 (14.5 oz.) can diced tomatoes, in liquid
2 (8 oz.) cans tomato sauce
2½ tsp. salt
¼ tsp. pepper
⅛ tsp. chili powder

Preheat the oven to 350°. Bring a large pot of lightly salted water to a boil. Add the mostaccioli and cook for 8 to 10 minutes or until tender. Drain water from pot and set aside. In a medium skillet over medium-high heat, cook ground beef, chopped onion and chopped celery until beef is browned and vegetables are tender. Drain the grease from the skillet. Add the diced tomatoes and liquid, tomato sauce, salt, pepper and chili powder. Pour the mixture into a 3-quart baking dish and bake in the oven for 30 minutes. To serve, spoon mixture onto separate dinner plates.

Mushroom Macaroni Bake

Makes 6 to 8 servings

1 (12 oz.) pkg. elbow macaroni
1 lb. ground beef
1 medium onion, chopped
1 C. chopped celery
1 (4 oz.) can sliced mushrooms, drained
1 (8 oz.) can whole kernel corn, drained
2 (10.75 oz.) cans cream of mushroom soup
1 C. milk
½ C. sour cream
½ C. shredded Cheddar cheese
½ tsp. seasoned salt
⅛ tsp. pepper

Preheat oven to 350°. Bring a large pot of lightly salted water to a boil. Add the elbow macaroni and cook for 8 to 10 minutes or until fully cooked. Drain and set aside. In a large skillet over medium-high heat, cook ground beef, chopped onion, chopped celery and mushrooms until beef is browned and vegetables are tender. Drain the grease from the skillet. In a medium bowl, mix together cream of mushroom soup, milk, sour cream, shredded Cheddar cheese, seasoned salt and pepper. Add the soup mixture to the ground beef mixture. Stir in the cooked elbow macaroni. Pour into a 3-quart baking dish. Cover and bake in the oven for 30 minutes. Uncover and bake 10 minutes more. To serve, spoon onto separate dinner plates.

Baked Zucchini and Beef

Makes 4 to 6 servings

5 T. olive oil, divided
3 lbs. sliced zucchini
1/3 C. chopped onion
1 lb. ground beef
1 (1.5 oz.) env. dry spaghetti sauce mix
1¾ C. water
1 (6 oz.) can tomato paste
¼ C. grated Parmesan cheese
1/3 C. dry bread crumbs
1 (8 oz.) pkg. shredded mozzarella cheese

Preheat the oven to 350°. In a medium skillet over medium-high heat, warm 3 tablespoons olive oil. Add the sliced zucchini and chopped onion; cook until tender. Place the vegetables in a 2-quart baking dish and set aside. In the same skillet over medium-high heat, cook the ground beef until browned. Drain the grease from the skillet. Add dry spaghetti sauce mix, water, tomato paste and remaining 2 tablespoons olive oil. Heat to a boil; reduce heat and let simmer for 10 minutes. Pour the mixture over the zucchini and onion. In a small bowl, mix together grated Parmesan cheese and bread crumbs. Sprinkle over the casserole and mix in gently. Top with shredded mozzarella cheese. Bake in the oven for 25 to 30 minutes or until topping is golden brown. To serve, spoon onto separate dinner plates.

Hamburger Biscuit Bake

Makes 4 to 6 servings

1 lb. ground beef
1 medium onion, chopped
1 green bell pepper, chopped
1 C. sliced mushrooms
1 (10.75 oz.) can Cheddar cheese soup
¾ C. milk
1 (8 oz.) tube refrigerated biscuits

Preheat the oven to 350°. In a medium skillet over medium-high heat, cook ground beef, chopped onion, chopped green bell pepper and sliced mushrooms until beef is browned and vegetables are tender. Drain the grease from the skillet. Stir in the Cheddar cheese soup and milk; cook until heated through. Press the biscuits into a single layer on the bottom of a greased 9 x 13" baking dish. Pour the hamburger mixture over the biscuits. Bake in the oven for 40 minutes. To serve, spoon onto separate dinner plates.

Cornbread Casserole

Makes 6 servings

1 lb. ground beef
1 tsp. dried oregano
¾ C. picante sauce
1 (8 oz.) can tomato sauce
1 (15.25 oz.) can whole kernel corn, drained
½ C. shredded Cheddar cheese
1 (8 oz.) pkg. corn muffin mix
Eggs and milk as directed on corn muffin mix package

Preheat the oven to 375°. In a medium skillet over medium-high heat, cook the ground beef and dried oregano until the beef is browned. Drain the grease from the skillet. Add the picante sauce, tomato sauce and whole kernel corn; cook until heated through. Stir in the shredded Cheddar cheese and pour into a 2-quart baking dish. Mix the corn muffin mix, eggs and milk according to the package directions. Spread the cornbread batter over the beef mixture. Bake in the oven for 25 to 30 minutes or until golden brown. Let stand 10 minutes before spooning onto individual dinner plates to serve.

Super Baked Ziti

3 C. uncooked ziti pasta
1 lb. ground beef
1 medium onion, chopped
1 (28 oz.) jar mushroom spaghetti sauce
1½ C. shredded mozzarella cheese, divided
¼ C. grated Parmesan cheese

Preheat the oven to 350°. Bring a large pot of lightly salted water to a boil. Add the ziti pasta and cook for 8 to 10 minutes or until tender. Drain water from pot and set aside. In a large saucepan over medium-high heat, cook the ground beef and onion until beef is browned and onion is tender. Drain the grease from the saucepan. Stir in the spaghetti sauce, 1 cup shredded mozzarella cheese and cooked ziti. Spoon the mixture into a 3-quart baking dish. Sprinkle the remaining ½ cup shredded mozzarella cheese and grated Parmesan cheese over the top. Bake in the oven for 30 minutes. To serve, spoon the baked ziti onto individual dinner plates.

Corn and Beef Pie

Makes 4 to 6 servings

1 lb. ground beef
¼ lb. ground sausage
1 small onion, chopped
1 clove garlic, minced
1 (15.25 oz.) can whole tomatoes, in liquid
1 (16 oz.) can whole kernel corn, drained
1 (2.25 oz.) can sliced black olives, drained
2 tsp. chili powder
1½ tsp. salt
1 C. cornmeal
1 C. milk
2 eggs, beaten
½ C. shredded Cheddar cheese

In a large skillet over medium-high heat, cook the ground beef, ground sausage, chopped onion and minced garlic until beef is browned and vegetables are tender. Drain the grease from the skillet. Add tomatoes and liquid, whole kernel corn, olives, chili powder and salt; heat to a boil. Pour the mixture into a 2-quart baking dish. In a medium bowl, mix together cornmeal, milk and eggs; pour over the meat mixture. Sprinkle the shredded Cheddar cheese over top and bake in the oven for 40 to 50 minutes or until golden brown. To serve, spoon the pie onto individual dinner plates.

Beef and Mashed Potato Pie

Makes 6 servings

4 medium potatoes
1 lb. ground beef
1 medium onion, chopped
2 (10.75 oz.) cans tomato soup
1 (15 oz.) can green beans, drained
1 C. shredded Cheddar cheese

Preheat the oven to 350°. Peel and quarter the potatoes. Bring a large pot of lightly salted water to a boil. Add the potatoes to the water, cover and cook for 15 minutes or until tender. Drain water from potatoes, mash and set aside. In a large skillet over medium-high heat, cook ground beef and onion until beef is browned and onion is tender. Drain the grease from the skillet. Stir in tomato soup and green beans. Pour the beef and bean mixture into a 9 x 13" baking dish. Spoon the mashed potatoes on top of the meat in mounds around the edge of the dish. Do not completely cover the meat. Sprinkle shredded Cheddar cheese over top of the mashed potatoes. Bake in the oven for 30 minutes or until potatoes are golden. To serve, spoon the pie onto individual dinner plates.

Biscuits-on-Top Bake

Makes 4 to 6 servings

1 lb. ground beef
1 small onion, chopped
2 medium potatoes, peeled and cubed
2 carrots, sliced
1½ C. brown gravy
1 (8 oz.) tube refrigerated biscuits
Salt and pepper to taste

Preheat the oven to 450°. In a medium skillet over medium-high heat, cook ground beef and chopped onion until beef is browned and onion is tender. Drain the grease from the skillet. Bring a pot of lightly salted water to a boil. Add the cubed potatoes and sliced carrots; cook until tender. Drain the water from the pot and add the ground beef. Season with salt and pepper and stir in the brown gravy. Place the mixture in a 2-quart baking dish and place the biscuits in a single layer over top. Bake in the oven for 15 to 20 minutes or until biscuits are cooked and golden. To serve, spoon the bake onto individual dinner plates.

Cheesy Ground Beef Quiche

Makes 6 servings

1 lb. ground beef
½ C. chopped onion
⅓ C. chopped green bell pepper
1½ C. shredded sharp Cheddar cheese
1 T. flour
1 deep dish pie crust, uncooked
2 eggs, beaten
1 C. evaporated milk
1 T. dried parsley
¾ tsp. seasoned salt
¼ tsp. garlic powder
¼ tsp. pepper

Preheat the oven to 375°. In a medium skillet over medium-high heat, cook the ground beef, chopped onion and chopped green bell pepper until the beef is browned and vegetables are tender. Drain the grease from the skillet. In a large bowl, combine the shredded sharp Cheddar cheese and flour. Stir the beef and vegetables into the cheese. Pour the entire mixture into the deep dish pie crust. In a medium bowl, whisk together eggs, evaporated milk, dried parsley, seasoned salt, garlic powder and pepper. Pour the egg mixture over the beef mixture. Bake for 35 to 40 minutes in the oven. To serve, slice quiche into six wedges.

Practically Pizza Casserole

Makes 6 servings

1 lb. ground beef
1 (8 oz.) can tomato sauce
4 to 6 slices American cheese
2 C. biscuit baking mix
$\frac{2}{3}$ C. milk

Preheat the oven to 450°. In a medium skillet over medium-high heat, cook ground beef until browned. Drain the grease from the skillet. Place beef in a 2-quart baking dish. Add the tomato sauce and top with a single layer of cheese slices. In a medium bowl, combine the biscuit baking mix with milk. Roll the dough and cut into thin biscuits. Place the biscuits in a single layer on top of the American cheese slices. Bake in the oven for 15 to 20 minutes or until biscuits are cooked and golden. To serve, spoon the casserole onto individual dinner plates.

Beef and Cheddar Cheese Pie

Makes 4 to 6 servings

1 lb. ground beef
²/₃ C. evaporated milk
¼ C. dry bread crumbs
1 tsp. garlic salt
¹/₃ C. ketchup
1 (3 oz.) can sliced mushrooms, drained
1 C. shredded Cheddar cheese
¼ tsp. dried oregano
2 T. grated Parmesan cheese
Paprika, to taste

Preheat the oven to 450°. In a medium bowl, combine the ground beef, evaporated milk, dry bread crumbs and garlic salt. Pat the mixture into the bottom and sides of a 9" pie pan. Spread the ketchup over the meat mixture and top with sliced mushrooms, Cheddar cheese, dried oregano, Parmesan cheese and paprika. Bake in the oven for 20 minutes or to desired doneness. To serve, cut the pie into wedges.

Onion and Beef Deep Dish Pie

Makes 4 to 6 servings

1 lb. ground beef
½ C. chopped onion
1 clove garlic, minced
1 (8 oz.) container sour cream
3 T. flour
½ tsp. dried thyme
¼ tsp. pepper
1 (10 oz.) pkg. frozen sweet peas with butter, thawed
1 frozen pre-rolled puff pastry sheet, thawed
1 egg, beaten

Preheat the oven to 400°. In a medium skillet over medium-high heat, cook ground beef, chopped onion and minced garlic until beef is browned and onion is tender. Drain the grease from the skillet. Stir in sour cream, flour, dried thyme and pepper. Fold in the sweet peas. Pour the mixture into a 1½-quart baking dish. Cut the pastry sheet to fit inside the top of the baking dish. Place it over the ground beef mixture and brush lightly with beaten egg. Use a fork to prick holes in the top of the pastry sheet. Bake in the oven for 25 to 35 minutes. To serve, spoon deep dish pie onto individual dinner plates.

Chili Pie

Makes 6 to 8 servings

1 lb. ground beef

1 medium green bell pepper, chopped

1 (16 oz.) can kidney beans, rinsed and drained

1 (14.5 oz.) can stewed tomatoes, cut up, in liquid

½ C. water

2 T. minced onion

1 T. chili powder

Dash of ground cinnamon

Dash of ground cloves

2 to 4 T. brown sugar, optional

½ C. mashed potato flakes

1 (15 oz.) frozen pastry for double crust pie, thawed

2 C. shredded Cheddar cheese, divided

1 T. butter, melted

1 T. sesame seeds

Shredded lettuce, optional

Preheat the oven to 400°. In a medium skillet over medium-high heat, cook ground beef and chopped green bell pepper until beef is browned and peppers are tender. Drain the grease from the skillet. Add the kidney beans, stewed tomatoes in liquid, water, minced onion, chili powder, ground cinnamon, ground cloves and brown sugar. Bring to a boil, reduce heat and let simmer for 12 to 15 minutes or until liquid is almost completely absorbed. Stir in the mashed potato flakes. On a floured surface, roll out one portion of the thawed pastry and shape to fit the bottom and sides of an ungreased 8" baking dish. Transfer pastry to dish and trim sides. Sprinkle ½ cup Cheddar cheese over the crust. Top with half the beef mixture and ¾ cup Cheddar cheese. Repeat with another layer of remaining beef and remaining ¾ cup Cheddar cheese. Roll out remaining pastry to fit inside the top of the dish over the cheese. Trim the edges and seal with a fork. Using the fork, prick holes in the top of the pastry crust. Brush with melted butter and sprinkle sesame seeds over top. Bake in the oven for 25 to 30 minutes or until golden brown. Let stand for 5 minutes before cutting into individual pieces and, if desired, serve with shredded lettuce.

Picadillo Pepper Casserole

Makes 4 servings

1 lb. ground beef
⅛ tsp. garlic powder
1 (14.5 oz.) can stewed tomatoes
½ C. picante sauce
1 tsp. ground cumin
¼ tsp. ground cinnamon
⅓ C. raisins
⅓ C. toasted slivered almonds*
2 medium green bell peppers, seeded
  and cut lengthwise into quarters
½ C. shredded Cheddar cheese
4 to 6 fresh basil leaves, optional

Preheat the oven to 350°. In a medium skillet over medium-high heat, cook ground beef and garlic until beef is browned; season with garlic powder. Add tomatoes, picante sauce, ground cumin, ground cinnamon, raisins and slivered almonds; cook until heated through. Arrange peppers in the bottom of a 2-quart baking dish. Spoon beef mixture over peppers; cover and cook for 25 minutes. Uncover and sprinkle shredded Cheddar cheese over top of the beef mixture and bake 5 minutes more or until cheese melts. To serve, spoon casserole onto individual dinner plates and, if desired, garnish with fresh basil leaves.

* To toast, place slivered almonds in a single layer on a baking sheet. Bake at 350° for approximately 10 minutes or until almonds are golden brown.

Tortilla Chip Casserole

Makes 4 to 6 servings

1 lb. ground beef
1 (4 oz.) can green chilies, drained
1 (9 oz.) bag lime tortilla chips, crushed
1 (10.75 oz.) can cream of mushroom soup
1 (2.25 oz.) can chopped olives, drained
3 C. shredded Cheddar cheese

Preheat oven to 350°. In a medium skillet over medium high heat, cook ground beef and chilies until beef is browned. Drain the grease from the skillet. In a large bowl, combine the tortilla chips, cream of mushroom soup, chopped olives and beef mixture. Pour mixture into a 9 x 13" baking dish and top with shredded Cheddar cheese. Bake for 15 minutes or until cheese is melted. To serve, spoon casserole onto individual serving plates.

Cheddar Noodle Beef Bake

1 (8 oz.) pkg. egg noodles
1 lb. ground beef
1 onion, chopped
2 (8 oz.) cans tomato sauce with mushrooms, divided
1 tsp. salt
¼ tsp. pepper
¼ tsp. ground cinnamon
1 C. cottage cheese
½ C. chopped green onions
½ C. shredded Cheddar cheese

Preheat oven to 350°. Bring a large pot of lightly salted water to a boil. Add egg noodles and cook for 8 to 10 minutes or until al dente. Drain water from pot and set aside. In a medium skillet over medium-high heat, cook ground beef and chopped onion until the beef is browned and onion is tender. Drain the grease from the skillet. Mix in one can of tomato sauce, salt, pepper and ground cinnamon. Pour into a shallow 3-quart baking dish. Spread noodles over the top in an even layer. Top with cottage cheese and sprinkle with green onions and shredded Cheddar cheese. Pour remaining can of tomato sauce over cheese. Bake in the oven for 30 minutes. To serve, spoon casserole onto individual dinner plates.

Beefy Mozzarella Casserole

Makes 4 servings

1 (16 oz.) pkg. spiral pasta
1 lb. ground beef
1 (28 oz.) jar spaghetti sauce
2 C. shredded mozzarella cheese, divided

Preheat the oven to 350°. Bring a large pot of lightly salted water to a boil. Add spiral pasta and cook for 8 to 10 minutes or until al dente. Drain water from pot and set aside. In a medium skillet over medium-high heat, cook ground beef until browned. Drain the grease from the skillet. Add spaghetti sauce and spiral pasta to beef. In a 3-quart baking dish, layer meat mixture and then shredded mozzarella cheese. Bake in the oven for 25 minutes. To serve, spoon casserole onto individual dinner plates.

Brunchy Broccoli Casserole

Makes 6 servings

1 lb. ground beef
1 (4 oz.) can mushrooms, drained
1 small onion, chopped
2 C. biscuit baking mix
2 C. shredded Cheddar cheese, divided
¼ C. grated Parmesan cheese
½ C. water
1 (10 oz.) pkg. frozen chopped broccoli, thawed and drained
4 eggs
½ C. milk
1 tsp. salt
Dash of pepper

Preheat the oven to 400°. In a medium skillet over medium-high heat, cook ground beef, mushrooms and chopped onion until beef is browned and onions are tender. Drain the grease from the skillet. In a medium bowl, combine biscuit baking mix, ½ cup shredded Cheddar cheese, Parmesan cheese and water until a soft dough forms. Press dough onto the bottom and ½" up the sides of a greased 9 x 13" baking dish. Stir remaining shredded Cheddar cheese into the beef mixture and spread it over dough. Sprinkle broccoli over the top. In a medium bowl, beat eggs, milk, salt and pepper. Pour eggs over meat mixture. Bake in the oven, uncovered, for 25 minutes or until a knife inserted near center comes out clean. To serve, spoon the casserole onto individual serving plates.

BEEFED UP

Main Dishes

Super-Duper Dinner Nachos

Makes 6 servings

1 lb. ground beef
1 small onion, chopped
1 (1 oz.) pkg. taco seasoning
1 (15 oz.) can tomato sauce
1 (15 oz.) can whole kernel corn, drained
2 (15 oz.) cans kidney beans, drained
6 C. tortilla chips
1 C. shredded Cheddar cheese
½ C. chopped green onions

In a medium skillet over medium-high heat, cook ground beef and chopped onion until beef is browned and onion is tender. Drain the grease from the skillet. In a slow cooker, combine the beef mixture, taco seasoning, tomato sauce, corn and kidney beans. Replace the lid and cook on low for 2 hours. For each serving, spread 1 cup of tortilla chips in a bowl, pour some taco mixture over the chips; sprinkle with Cheddar cheese and chopped green onions.

Green Peppers and Ground Beef

Makes 4 to 6 servings

1 lb. ground beef
1 small onion, diced
1 green bell pepper, diced
1 tsp. garden or nature blend* seasoned salt
1 (14.5 oz.) can whole tomatoes, drained and chopped
½ tsp. pepper

In a medium skillet over medium-high heat, cook ground beef, diced onions and diced green pepper until beef is browned and vegetables are tender. Drain the grease from the skillet. Add seasoned salt, chopped tomatoes and pepper; mix well. Cover and let simmer for 20 minutes. To serve, spoon mixture onto individual dinner plates.

*Garden or nature blend seasoned salt generally includes a mixture of onion, garlic, salt, pepper and other natural spices.

Super Simple Meatballs

Makes 2 to 4 servings

1 lb. ground beef
½ C. uncooked rice
½ tsp. salt
¼ tsp. pepper
2 T. chopped onion
1 (10.75 oz.) can tomato soup
Cooked rice or pasta, optional

Preheat the oven to 350°. In a large bowl, mix together ground beef, uncooked rice, salt, pepper and chopped onion. Form the mixture into 12 meatballs about 1" in diameter. Place the meatballs in a greased 9 x 13" baking dish and pour the tomato soup over them. Bake in the oven for 1 hour or until internal temperature of meatballs reaches 160°. Serve meatballs over a bed of pasta or rice, if desired.

Cheesy Meatloaf

Makes 6 servings

1 lb. ground beef
½ T. pepper
¾ C. cubed Cheddar cheese
½ T. celery seed
½ medium onion, chopped
¼ T. paprika
½ medium green bell pepper, chopped
½ C. milk
1 egg, beaten
½ C. dry bread crumbs

Preheat the oven to 350°. In a large bowl, mix together the ground beef, pepper, cubed Cheddar cheese, celery seed, chopped onion, paprika, chopped green bell pepper, milk, egg and dry bread crumbs. Form the mixture into a loaf and place in 2-quart baking dish. Bake in the oven for 1 hour and 15 minutes or until internal temperature of meatloaf reaches 160°. To serve, slice the loaf into six pieces.

Snappy Apple-Glazed Meatloaf

Makes 10 servings

1 onion, minced
2 C. soft bread crumbs
2 C. applesauce, divided
1 egg, beaten
$\frac{1}{8}$ tsp. pepper
1 lb. ground beef
1 lb. ground pork
2 T. apple cider vinegar
1 T. Dijon mustard
2 T. brown sugar

Preheat the oven to 350°. In a microwave-safe bowl, cook minced onion in microwave for 2 to 3 minutes or until tender. In a large bowl, combine onion, bread crumbs, 1 cup applesauce, egg and pepper. Stir in beef and pork and gently mix. Shape mixture into loaf and place in a 2-quart baking dish. In a medium saucepan over medium heat, combine the remaining 1 cup of applesauce, apple cider vinegar, Dijon mustard and brown sugar. Cook until heated through. Bake the meatloaf in the oven for 1 hour and 30 minutes or until internal temperature of meatloaf reaches 160°. Baste the meatloaf with the glaze every 20 minutes. Let meatloaf cool for 15 minutes before slicing and serving.

Sesame Barbecued Meatballs

Makes 4 to 6 servings

1 lb. ground beef
⅓ C. minced green onions
¼ C. chopped onion
3 T. soy sauce
2 T. sesame seeds, toasted*
1 T. sugar
1 T. vegetable oil
Steamed rice, optional

Preheat the grill to medium-high heat. In a medium bowl, combine the ground beef, minced green onions, chopped onion, soy sauce, toasted sesame seeds, sugar and vegetable oil. Shape mixture into 12 meatballs about 1" in diameter. Transfer meatballs to a 10 x 15" baking pan, cover and chill in the refrigerator for 1 hour. Soak six wooden skewers in water for 30 minutes. Thread two meatballs on each skewer. Cook meatballs on the grill for 6 to 8 minutes on each side or until meat is no longer pink and internal temperature reaches 160°. Serve meatballs over a bed of steamed rice if desired.

*To toast, place sesame seeds in a single layer on a baking sheet. Bake at 350° for approximately 10 minutes or until sesame seeds are golden brown.

Creamy Pasta and Beef

Makes 4 servings

1 lb. ground beef
1 medium onion, chopped
1 (10.75 oz.) can cream of celery soup
¼ C. ketchup
1 T. Worcestershire sauce
2 C. cooked spiral pasta

In a medium skillet over medium-high heat, cook ground beef and chopped onion until beef is browned and onion is tender. Drain the grease from the skillet. Add cream of celery soup, ketchup, Worcestershire sauce and cooked pasta. Cook, stirring occasionally, until heated through. To serve, spoon mixture onto individual dinner plates.

Taco Skillet

Makes 4 servings

1 lb. ground beef
1 (10.75 oz.) can tomato soup
1 C. salsa
½ C. water
8 (8") flour tortillas, cut into 1" pieces
1 C. shredded Cheddar cheese, divided

In a medium skillet over medium-high heat, cook ground beef until browned. Drain the grease from the skillet. Add tomato soup, salsa, water, tortillas and ½ cup shredded Cheddar cheese; heat to a boil. Cover and cook over low heat for 5 minutes or until cooked through. To serve, spoon mixture onto individual dinner plates and top with remaining shredded Cheddar cheese.

Southwestern Potato Topper

1 lb. ground beef
1 (10.75 oz.) can Cheddar cheese soup
1 C. salsa
4 hot baked potatoes, split
Sour cream, optional
Sliced black olives, optional

In a medium skillet over medium-high heat, cook ground beef until browned. Drain the grease from the skillet. Add Cheddar cheese soup and salsa; cook until heated through. To serve, spoon ¼ of the mixture over each baked potato half and, if desired, top with sour cream and sliced olives.

Beefy Bean Burritos

Makes 8 servings

1 lb. ground beef
1 small onion, chopped
1 (11.25 oz.) can fiesta chili beef soup
¼ C. water
8 (8") flour tortillas, warmed
1 C. shredded Cheddar cheese, divided
½ C. salsa
Sour cream, optional

In a medium skillet over medium-high heat, cook ground beef and chopped onion until beef is browned and onion is tender. Drain the grease from the skillet. Add fiesta chili beef soup and water; cook until heated through. Spoon a portion of the meat mixture into the center of each tortilla. Top with shredded Cheddar cheese, salsa and sour cream, if desired. To serve, fold the tortilla around the filling.

Slow Cooker Cabbage Rolls

Makes 6 servings

12 large cabbage leaves
1 egg, beaten
¼ C. milk
¼ C. minced onion
1 tsp. salt
¼ tsp. pepper
1 lb. ground beef
1 C. cooked white rice
1 (8 oz.) can tomato sauce
1 T. brown sugar
1 T. lemon juice
1 tsp. Worcestershire sauce

In a pot of boiling water, cook cabbage leaves for 3 minutes or until limp. Drain water from pot. In a medium bowl, combine egg, milk, minced onion, salt, pepper, ground beef and cooked rice. Spoon ¼ of the mixture into the center of each cooked cabbage leaf. Fold the sides and ends of each cabbage leaf over the filling. Place the cabbage leaves in a slow cooker. In a medium bowl, combine tomato sauce, brown sugar, lemon juice and Worcestershire sauce. Pour the mixture over the cabbage rolls and cook on low for 7 to 9 hours. To serve, place two cabbage rolls on each individual dinner plate.

Upside-Down Bacon Burger Pizza

Makes 6 to 8 servings

1 lb. ground beef
1 medium onion, sliced
1 medium green bell pepper, cut into strips
8 slices crisp cooked bacon, crumbled, divided
1 (14.5 oz.) can chunky pizza sauce
3 Italian plum tomatoes, chopped
4 oz. Cheddar cheese, sliced
2 eggs
1 C. milk
1 T. vegetable oil
1 C. flour
¼ tsp. salt

Preheat the oven to 400°. In a medium saucepan over medium-high heat, cook ground beef, sliced onion and green bell pepper until beef is browned and vegetables are tender. Drain the grease from the skillet. Stir in six slices of the crumbled bacon and chunky pizza sauce. Spoon mixture in a 9 x 13" baking dish. Sprinkle chopped tomatoes over top of the beef mixture and top with sliced Cheddar cheese. In a medium bowl, beat eggs. Add milk and vegetable oil to the eggs. Add the flour and salt and beat with a mixer for 2 minutes at medium speed. Pour the mixture over the cheese and sprinkle remaining two slices of crumbled bacon over top. Bake in the oven for 20 to 30 minutes or until topping is puffed and golden brown. To serve, spoon upside-down pizza onto individual dinner plates.

Moroccan Beef and Beans

Makes 4 servings

1 (10 oz.) box couscous
1 lb. ground beef
1 tsp. salt
½ tsp. pepper
1½ tsp. minced garlic
1 (15 oz.) can diced tomatoes, in liquid
¾ lb. green beans, trimmed and cut in half
1 C. diced carrots
1 T. chopped fresh mint

Bring a large pot of lightly salted water to a boil. Add couscous and stir. Bring to a boil again, lower heat and cover. Simmer until all the water has been absorbed. Stir to fluff, remove from heat and allow to stand 5 minutes; set aside. In a medium skillet over medium-high heat, cook ground beef, salt and pepper until beef is browned. Drain the grease from the skillet. Add minced garlic and let cook 1 minute more. Add tomatoes and liquid, green beans and carrots; bring to a boil. Reduce heat and simmer for 15 minutes. Stir in mint. Divide meat mixture between four shallow serving bowls and serve with couscous.

Beef Teriyaki Lettuce Wraps

Makes 4 servings

1 head lettuce
2 large carrots, shredded
1 large green bell pepper, cut into thin strips
4 T. rice wine vinegar, divided
¼ tsp. salt
1 lb. ground beef
4 T. roasted garlic teriyaki marinade, divided
1 jalapeno pepper, seeded and minced
1 T. water

Core lettuce and remove eight whole lettuce leaves; set aside. Slice up 1 cup of the remaining lettuce. In a large bowl, toss together sliced lettuce, shredded carrots, green bell pepper, 3 tablespoons rice wine vinegar and salt. In a medium bowl, mix ground beef with 3 tablespoons roasted garlic teriyaki marinade. Shape the beef into 20 to 24 ½"-square pieces. In a large skillet over medium-high heat, cook the beef pieces, turning until browned on all sides. Add the minced jalapeno, water, remaining 1 tablespoon of rice wine vinegar and 1 tablespoon roasted garlic teriyaki marinade. Bring to a simmer, cover and cook for 3 minutes. Spoon a portion of the beef mixture and a portion of the salad mixture into each lettuce leaf and close the leaf around the filling. To serve, place each lettuce wrap on individual dinner plates.

Cheddar Cheese Tacos

1 lb. ground beef
1 (10.75 oz.) can Cheddar cheese soup
½ C. chunky salsa
8 (8") flour tortillas, warmed
2 C. shredded lettuce

In a medium skillet over medium-high heat, cook ground beef until browned. Drain the grease from the skillet. Add Cheddar cheese soup and chunky salsa. Reduce heat to low and cook until heated throughout. Spoon ⅓ cup of the mixture into the center of each tortilla. To serve, top with shredded lettuce and fold or roll the tortilla around the filling.

Ground Beef Chow Mein

Makes 4 to 6 servings

¼ C. butter
1 lb. ground beef
1 medium onion, chopped
1½ tsp. salt
⅛ tsp. pepper
2 C. chopped celery
1½ C. water
3 T. cornstarch
1½ T. soy sauce
1 tsp. sugar
1 T. prepared brown gravy
2 (14 oz.) cans bean sprouts, rinsed and drained
1 (4 oz.) can mushrooms, drained
1 (5 oz.) can chow mein noodles

In a medium skillet over medium-high heat, warm the butter. Add the ground beef and chopped onion; cook until beef is browned and onion is tender. Add salt, pepper, chopped celery and water. Cover and let simmer for 20 minutes. In a medium bowl, blend the cornstarch with a little cold water. Add the soy sauce, sugar and gravy. Stir mixture into the ground beef. Add the bean sprouts and mushrooms and cook until thickened. Serve beef mixture hot over a bed of chow mein noodles.

Microwave Enchilada Torte

Makes 6 servings

1 lb. ground beef
1 (16 oz.) jar chunky salsa
1 T. chili powder
8 (8") flour tortillas
1 (10.75 oz.) Cheddar cheese soup
1 C. shredded Cheddar cheese
Sour cream, optional

In a medium skillet over medium-high heat, cook ground beef until browned. Drain the grease from the skillet. Add salsa and chili powder to beef. In shallow 2-quart, microwave-safe baking dish, layer four of the tortillas across the bottom. Top tortillas with half the meat mixture and half the soup. Place the remaining four tortillas on top of the soup and top with the remaining meat and soup. Sprinkle shredded Cheddar cheese over top and cover with a lid. Cook in the microwave at medium-high setting for 8 minutes or until hot. To serve, cut torte into pieces and place on individual dinner plates. Top with sour cream, if desired.

Mozzarella Beef Patties and Pasta

Makes 4 servings

1 lb. ground beef
2 C. spaghetti sauce
4 slices mozzarella cheese
4 C. cooked spaghetti

Shape ground beef into four patties. In a large skillet over medium-high heat, cook patties until browned on both sides. Drain the grease from the skillet. Add spaghetti sauce and heat to a boil. Reduce to low, cover and cook for 5 minutes or until simmering. Top each patty with one slice of mozzarella cheese, cover and heat until cheese melts. Serve each patty over 1 cup of cooked spaghetti.

Savory Salisbury Steak

1 lb. ground beef
⅓ C. dry bread crumbs
1 small onion, minced
1 egg, beaten
2 T. water
1 T. vegetable oil
1 (10.25 oz.) can beef gravy

In a medium bowl, mix ground beef, dry bread crumbs, minced onion, egg and water. Shape beef mixture into four hamburger patties. In a medium skillet over medium-high heat, warm vegetable oil. Add patties and cook until browned on both sides. Drain the grease from the skillet. Add beef gravy and heat to a boil. Reduce heat to low, cover and cook 10 minutes or until patties are fully cooked. Serve each Salisbury steak on an individual dinner plate and spoon some of the gravy from the skillet over top.

Vegetable Beef Packs

1 lb. ground beef
1 (15.25 oz.) can whole kernel corn, drained
1 (15.25 oz.) can green beans, drained
2 (4 oz.) cans mushrooms, drained
1 (16 oz.) jar processed cheese sauce
Salt and pepper to taste

Preheat the oven to 350°. Cut out four squares of aluminum foil. Form ground beef into four patties. Place each patty in the center of a piece of aluminum foil. Top each burger with some of the whole kernel corn, green beans, mushrooms and 1 tablespoon of processed cheese sauce. Fold foil over patty and seal. Bake in the oven for 1 hour. Remove from oven and open foil packets. To serve, place the contents of each packet on an individual dinner plate.

Spanish Rice and Beef

Makes 8 servings

1 C. uncooked brown rice
1¼ C. water
1 tsp. butter
1 lb. ground beef
1 medium onion, chopped
1 (28 oz.) can stewed tomatoes, in liquid
1 tsp. celery salt
1 tsp. salt
1 tsp. honey
½ tsp. garlic salt
½ tsp. pepper
1 C. shredded Cheddar cheese

Preheat the oven to 350°. In a medium saucepan over medium-high heat, combine rice, water and butter; bring to a boil. Reduce heat, cover and let simmer 10 to 12 minutes or until water is absorbed. Fluff with a fork and set aside. In a medium skillet over medium-high heat, cook ground beef and chopped onion until beef is browned and onion is tender. Drain the grease from the skillet. Stir in stewed tomatoes and liquid, celery salt, salt, honey, garlic salt, pepper and cooked rice. Transfer mixture to a greased 2-quart baking dish. Cover and bake for 50 to 55 minutes. Remove from oven and sprinkle Cheddar cheese over top. Bake, uncovered, 5 to 10 minutes more or until cheese is melted. To serve, spoon mixture on individual dinner plates.

Quickie Beef Pizza

Makes 4 to 6 servings

1 lb. ground beef
1 (10.75 oz.) can cream of mushroom soup
1 (12") pre-baked thin pizza crust
1 (8 oz.) pkg. shredded Cheddar cheese

Preheat the oven to 425°. In a medium skillet over medium-high heat, cook ground beef until browned. Drain the grease from the skillet. Spread cream of mushroom soup over the pre-baked pizza crust. Spread cooked beef over the soup and sprinkle shredded Cheddar cheese over top. Bake in the oven for 15 minutes or until cheese is melted and bubbly. To serve, cut pizza into four to six wedges.

Meaty Manicotti

Makes 8 servings

2 (8 oz.) pkgs. manicotti shells
1 lb. ground beef
1 lb. pork sausage
1 C. chopped sweet onion
2 tsp. minced garlic
½ C. Italian seasoned dry bread crumbs
2 T. chopped fresh parsley
2 tsp. dried oregano
2 (16 oz.) jars spaghetti sauce, divided
2 C. shredded mozzarella cheese

Bring a large pot of lightly salted water to a boil. Add manicotti shells and cook until tender. Drain water from pot and set aside. Preheat the oven to 375°. In a medium skillet over medium-high heat, cook the beef and pork until browned. Drain the grease from the skillet and transfer meat to a bowl. Place onion and garlic in the skillet, and cook until onion is tender. Transfer to bowl with beef. Mix the Italian seasoned bread crumbs, chopped fresh parsley and dried oregano into the bowl. Spread half the pasta sauce over the bottom of a 9 x 13" baking dish. Stuff manicotti shells with the meat mixture and arrange on top of the sauce. Pour the remaining sauce over the stuffed shells. Cover dish with foil and bake manicotti in the oven for 40 minutes. Remove from oven, uncover, sprinkle with shredded mozzarella cheese, and continue baking 20 minutes or until cheese is bubbly. To serve, spoon manicotti onto individual dinner plates.

Hashbrown Hamburger

Makes 4 servings

1 lb. ground beef
1 large onion, chopped
3 potatoes, peeled and cubed
2 T. beef bouillon
Water to cover

In a large saucepan over medium-high heat, cook ground beef and chopped onion until beef is browned and onion is tender. Drain the grease from the saucepan. Add cubed potatoes, bouillon and enough water to cover the ingredients. Cover saucepan, reduce heat and let simmer for 30 minutes or until potatoes are tender and water has evaporated. To serve, spoon onto individual dinner plates.

Italian Enchiladas

Makes 10 servings

1 lb. ground beef
1 small onion, chopped
1 (10.75 oz.) can cream of mushroom soup
½ (1 lb.) loaf processed cheese, cut into thin slices
1 (26 oz.) can marinara sauce
1 (8 oz.) can tomato sauce
¼ C. plus 2 T. water
10 (10") flour tortillas

Preheat the oven to 350°. In a medium skillet over medium-high heat, cook ground beef and chopped onion until beef is browned and onion is tender. Drain the grease from the skillet. Mix in cream of mushroom soup and continue cooking until heated through. In a large bowl, mix the marinara sauce, tomato sauce and water. Spread ⅓ of the sauce mixture across the bottom of a 9 x 13" baking pan. Fill each tortilla with about 2 tablespoons of beef mixture and 2 slices of processed cheese. Tightly roll each tortilla. Arrange 2 layers of tortillas in a baking pan and cover completely with the remaining sauce mixture. Top with a layer of the remaining processed cheese slices. Cover with aluminum foil and bake in the oven for 45 minutes or until bubbly. To serve, place each enchilada on an individual dinner plate.

Mozzarella Spinach Meatloaf

Makes 8 servings

1 lb. ground beef
1 (10 oz.) pkg. frozen chopped spinach, thawed and drained
1½ C. Italian seasoned dry bread crumbs
2 C. shredded mozzarella cheese, divided
2 eggs, beaten

Preheat oven to 350°. In a large bowl, mix the ground beef, chopped spinach, Italian seasoned bread crumbs, 1½ cups shredded mozzarella cheese and eggs. Transfer the mixture to a greased 5 x 9" loaf pan. Bake in the oven for 1 hour or to an internal temperature of 160°. Top meatloaf with remaining ½ cup shredded mozzarella cheese. To serve, slice the meatloaf into eight pieces.

Fake Fillets

Makes 6 servings

1 lb. ground beef
¾ C. dry bread crumbs
2 eggs, beaten
2 T. chopped onion
1½ tsp. salt
⅛ tsp. pepper
6 slices bacon
½ C. ketchup
2 T. brown sugar
¼ tsp. dry mustard

Preheat the broiler. In a medium bowl, mix ground beef and bread crumbs. Add eggs, chopped onion, salt and pepper. Shape the mixture into 6 patties. Wrap one piece of bacon around the outside rim of each patty; secure with toothpicks. Place the filets on a rack in a broiler pan or casserole dish and broil 5" from heat source for 10 minutes. Remove from the oven and turn patties over. In a small bowl mix ketchup, brown sugar and mustard. Spoon mixture over patties and broil for 5 minutes more or to desired doneness. To serve, place each fillet on an individual dinner plate.

Beefy Carrot Skillet

Makes 4 to 6 servings

1 lb. ground beef
1 (1 oz.) pkg. onion soup mix
4½ C. boiling water
2 beef bouillon cubes
¼ C. dried parsley
1 C. sliced carrots
1 (8 oz.) pkg. spiral pasta

In medium skillet over medium-high heat, cook ground beef until browned. Drain the grease from the skillet. Add onion soup mix, boiling water, beef bouillon cubes, dried parsley and sliced carrots. Let simmer for 15 minutes. Add spiral pasta and simmer until noodles are tender. To serve, spoon mixture onto individual dinner plates.

Simple Beef Stroganoff

1 lb. ground beef
1 small onion, chopped
½ tsp. garlic salt
¼ tsp. pepper
1 (10.75 oz.) can cream of mushroom soup
1 (4 oz.) can mushrooms, drained
¾ C. sour cream
Cooked rice or pasta, optional

In a medium skillet over medium-high heat, cook ground beef and chopped onion until beef is browned and onion is tender. Drain the grease from the skillet. Stir in garlic salt, pepper, cream of mushroom soup and mushrooms. Cover and simmer for 15 to 20 minutes. Stir in sour cream and cook until heated through. Do not boil. Serve stroganoff over a bed of rice or pasta.

Petite Meatloaves

Makes 8 servings

1 egg
¾ C. milk
1 C. shredded Cheddar cheese
½ C. quick-cooking oats
1 tsp. salt
1 lb. ground beef
⅔ C. ketchup
¼ C. brown sugar
1½ tsp. mustard

Preheat the oven to 350°. In a large bowl, combine the egg, milk, shredded Cheddar cheese, quick-cooking oats and salt. Add the ground beef and form the mixture into eight small meatloaves. Place meatloaves into a greased 9 x 13" baking dish. In a small bowl, combine the ketchup, brown sugar and mustard. Pour the mixture over each small meatloaf. Bake in the oven, uncovered, for 45 minutes or until an internal temperature of 160° is reached. To serve, place each meatloaf on an individual dinner plate.

Honey and Eggplant Beef Skillet

Makes 4 to 6 servings

1 lb. ground beef
1 medium eggplant, diced
Salt and pepper to taste
3 T. miso paste
½ C. warm water
3 T. honey
1 T. crushed dried chilies
2 T. vinegar
5 to 6 green onions, chopped
Soy sauce, optional

In a medium skillet over medium-high heat, cook ground beef until browned. Drain the grease from the skillet. Stir in diced eggplant and season with salt and pepper. Cover and cook until eggplant is tender. In a small bowl, mix miso paste with warm water; add to eggplant and beef. Stir in honey and crushed dried chilies. Gently stir in vinegar and let simmer 10 to 15 minutes, stirring often. Add chopped green onions and soy sauce, if desired. To serve, spoon mixture onto individual dinner plates.

Beefed Up Pork and Beans

Makes 4 to 6 servings

1 lb. ground beef
½ medium onion, chopped
½ medium green bell pepper, chopped
3 (16 oz.) cans pork and beans
1 T. brown sugar
½ C. ketchup

In a medium skillet over medium-high heat, cook ground beef, chopped onions and chopped green bell pepper until beef is browned and vegetables are tender. In a medium pot over low heat, combine beef mixture, pork and beans, brown sugar and ketchup. Cover and simmer for 15 minutes, stirring occasionally. To serve, spoon mixture onto individual dinner plates.

Broccoli Beef Wraps

Makes 4 servings

1 lb. ground beef
¼ C. finely chopped onion
½ tsp. salt
¼ tsp. pepper
3 C. chopped broccoli
¼ C. hoisin sauce
4 (10") tortillas, warmed

In a medium skillet over medium-high heat, cook ground beef and chopped onion until beef is browned and onion is tender. Drain the grease from the skillet and season beef with salt and pepper. Stir in chopped broccoli and hoisin sauce; cook until heated through. Spread 1 cup of the beef mixture on the center of each tortilla and fold edges around the filling or roll tortillas. Place each wrap on individual dinner plates and serve with additional hoisin sauce, if desired.

Cajun Beef and Dirty Rice

Makes 4 servings

1 lb. ground beef
1 medium green bell pepper, chopped
2½ C. water
1 (8 oz.) pkg. Cajun-style dirty rice mix
1 (14.5 oz.) can diced tomatoes, drained

In a medium skillet over medium-high heat, cook ground beef and chopped green pepper until beef is browned and green peppers are tender. Drain the grease from the skillet. In a medium pot, bring water to a boil. Add Cajun-style dirty rice and return to a boil. Reduce heat and let simmer for 20 to 25 minutes or until water is evaporated. Add cooked rice and diced tomatoes to beef and cook until heated through, stirring occasionally. To serve, spoon mixture onto individual dinner plates.

Mexican Stuffed Acorn Squash

Makes 4 servings

1 acorn squash
1 lb. ground beef
1 medium onion, chopped
1 T. taco seasoning
¼ tsp. ground cinnamon
1 (8 oz.) can tomato sauce
⅓ C. raisins
1 T. slivered almonds, optional

Preheat the oven to 375°. Cut the acorn squash into quarters and scoop out the seeds. Place the squash pieces on a greased baking sheet and bake in the oven for 45 minutes or until tender. In a medium skillet over medium-high heat, cook ground beef until browned. Drain the grease from the skillet. Sprinkle taco seasoning and cinnamon over beef. Stir in tomato sauce and raisins; bring to a boil. Reduce heat, cover and simmer for 15 minutes, stirring occasionally. To serve, place each quarter of cooked acorn squash on a plate and top with beef mixture. Garnish with slivered almonds, if desired.

Biscuit Bubble Pizza

1 lb. ground beef
¼ lb. sliced pepperoni sausage
1 (14 oz.) can pizza sauce
2 (12 oz.) pkgs. refrigerated biscuits
½ medium onion, sliced
2 (4.25 oz.) cans sliced black olives
1 (4 oz.) can mushrooms, drained
1½ C. shredded mozzarella cheese
1 C. shredded Cheddar cheese

Preheat the oven to 400°. In a medium skillet over medium-high heat, cook ground beef until browned. Add sliced pepperoni sausage and cook until heated. Drain the grease from the skillet. Stir in pizza sauce and remove from heat; set aside. Cut biscuits into quarters and place in the bottom of a greased 9 x 13" baking dish. Spread meat mixture evenly over the biscuits. Sprinkle sliced onion, sliced black olives and sliced mushrooms over the meat mixture. Bake, uncovered, in the oven for 20 to 25 minutes. Remove from the oven and sprinkle mozzarella and Cheddar cheese over the top. Bake an additional 5 to 10 minutes or until cheese is melted. To serve, cut into square pieces and place on individual dinner plates.

Mexican Macaroni

Makes 4 servings

1½ C. uncooked elbow macaroni

1 lb. ground beef

1 C. picante sauce

1 T. chili powder

1 (14.5 oz.) can whole peeled tomatoes,
  drained and chopped

1 C. frozen whole kernel corn

½ C. shredded Cheddar cheese

Sliced avocado, optional

Sour cream, optional

Bring a large pot of lightly salted water to a boil. Add uncooked elbow macaroni and cook for 8 to 10 minutes or until fully cooked. Drain the water from the pot and set aside. In a medium skillet over medium-high heat, cook ground beef until browned. Drain the grease from the skillet. Add picante sauce, chili powder and whole kernel corn. Reduce heat to low and cook for 10 minutes. Stir in cooked pasta and sprinkle shredded Cheddar cheese over top. Cover and heat until cheese melts. To serve, spoon mixture onto individual dinner plates and garnish with sliced avocado and sour cream, if desired.

Slow-Cooked Pizza

Makes 6 servings

1 (8 oz.) pkg. rigatoni pasta
1 lb. ground beef
1 (16 oz.) pkg. shredded mozzarella cheese
1 (10.75 oz.) can tomato soup
2 (14 oz.) jars pizza sauce
1 (8 oz.) pkg. sliced pepperoni sausage

Bring a large pot of lightly salted water to a boil. Add rigatoni pasta and cook for 8 to 10 minutes or until al dente; drain and set aside. In a medium skillet over medium-high heat, cook ground beef until browned. Drain the grease from the skillet. In a slow cooker, layer half the ground beef, half the noodles, half the shredded mozzarella cheese, half the tomato soup, half the pizza sauce and half the pepperoni. Repeat layers with remaining ingredients. Replace lid and cook on low for 4 hours. To serve, spoon slow-cooked pizza onto individual dinner plates.

Sauerbraten Beef Balls

Makes 4 servings

1 lb. ground beef
¼ C. milk
¼ C. dry bread crumbs
⅛ tsp. ground cloves
⅛ tsp. ground allspice
½ tsp. salt
½ tsp. pepper
2 T. vegetable oil
1 C. water
½ C. white vinegar
¼ C. brown sugar
¾ tsp. ground ginger
1 bay leaf
2 T. flour

In a large bowl, mix together ground beef, milk and dry bread crumbs. Season beef mixture with ground cloves, ground allspice, salt and pepper. Shape the mixture into 12 meatballs about 1" in diameter. Heat vegetable oil in a large heavy skillet over medium heat. Cook the meatballs in the skillet until evenly browned. Drain the grease from the skillet. Stir in 1 cup of water, white vinegar, brown sugar, ground ginger and bay leaf. Cover the skillet and simmer for 30 minutes. Skim fat off the meatballs. Transfer meatballs to a serving dish and keep warm. In a small saucepan over medium heat, combine flour with 2 tablespoons of water and whisk until well combined. Cook flour mixture over medium heat, stirring constantly, until thickened. Before serving, pour gravy over meatballs.

Index

Beefing Up Your Knowledge

Beefed Up Soups and Stews

Beefed Up Burgers and Sandwiches

Beefed Up Casseroles, Bakes and Pies

Beefed Up Main Dishes